# Queen Victoria

## THE LONGEST REIGNING ENGLISH MONARCH

Biography 3rd Grade
Children's Biography Books

BABY PROFESSOR
EDUCATION KIDS

Speedy Publishing LLC

40 E. Main St. #1156

Newark, DE 19711

www.speedypublishing.com

Copyright 2017

In this book, we're going to talk about the life of Queen Victoria. So, let's get right to it!

# WHO WAS QUEEN VICTORIA?

Queen Victoria was the ruler of Great Britain and Ireland from June of 1837 to her death in January of 1901. From the year 1876 though 1901, she was also the Empress of India. She ruled for over 63 years, which was the longest reign for any English monarch.

QUEEN VICTORIA

CRYSTAL PALACE, 1851

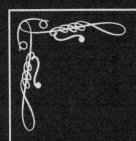
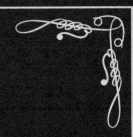

Victoria's time as Queen of England came to be called the "Victorian Era." This era was known for its strict moral principles. Under her leadership, the United Kingdom became a world power. During her reign, there was huge progress in communication as well as industry and technology. Transportation also made enormous leaps forward as many of the railways that were built underground date back to the Victorian Era.

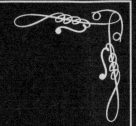

ridges, roads, and above ground railways that still form the infrastructure of the United Kingdom today were built when Queen Victoria ruled. In addition to the progress made in these areas, the Queen was responsible for ushering in progress in human society as well.

THE LOUTH-LONDON ROYAL
MAIL TRAVELING BY TRAIN
FROM PETERBOROUGH

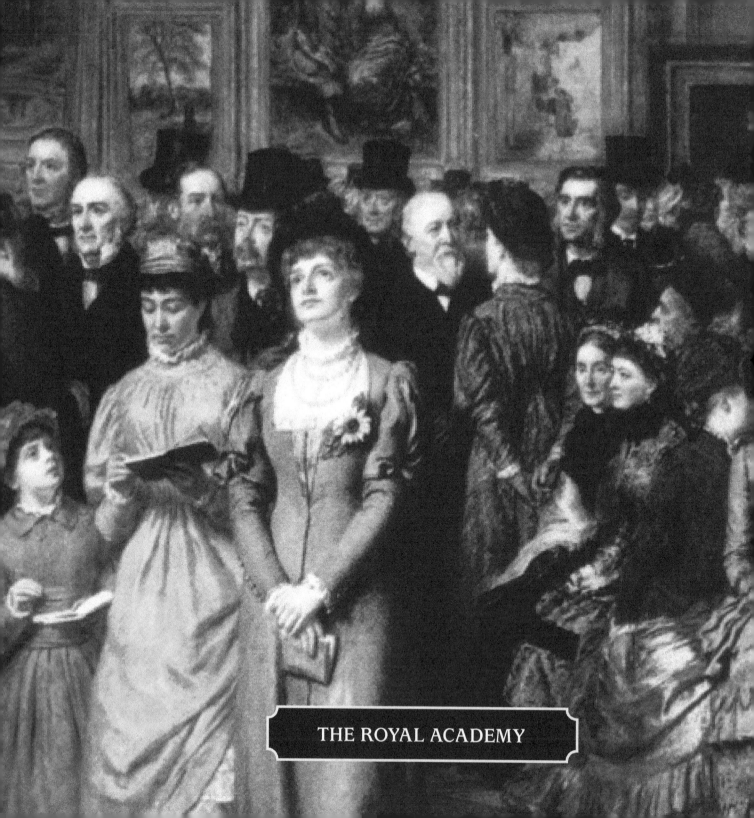

THE ROYAL ACADEMY

She did much to decrease poverty and to reduce the differences among the social classes. She was an advocate for literacy and during her rule the United Kingdom made strides in making most of its citizens literate.

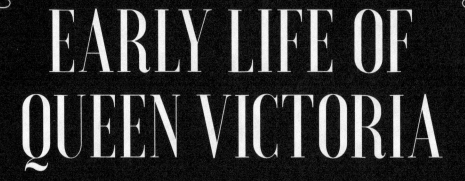

# EARLY LIFE OF QUEEN VICTORIA

P rior to Queen Victoria's birth, King George III ruled the United Kingdom. He had seven sons and George IV was the son who was the Prince Regent, which means he was in line for the throne. George IV had a daughter but no sons. Unfortunately, his daughter, Princess Charlotte of Wales, passed away during childbirth. When this happened, the other sons of George III all sought to have a child so that the first child born would be a direct heir to the throne.

KING GEORGE III

KENSINGTON PALACE, 1819

The Duke of Kent, Prince Edward Augustus, and his wife Victoria, who came from Germany, were the parents of Princess Victoria. She was born on the 24th of May in the year 1819 in London at the Kensington Palace. She was baptized by the Archbishop of Canterbury and was given the name Alexandrina Victoria. As she got older she was nicknamed "Drina."

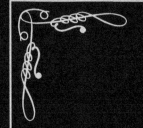
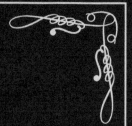

To begin with, it didn't appear that Victoria would become Queen. She was fifth in line for the throne after her father and her uncles. However, after her father and grandfather passed away when she was only 1-year-old, Victoria became the heiress to her uncle, the Duke of Clarence, who was also called William IV. He assumed the responsibility of guardianship until she became an adult at age 18.

WILLIAM IV OF GREAT BRITAIN

As she grew up, she was protected and sheltered. As any royal, she had to live by very detailed rules and regal protocols.

She was often sad because she was not allowed to meet anyone new. She didn't go to school like normal commoners.

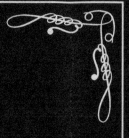

She was tutored at home instead. She studied the European languages as well as Latin. When her classes were over for the day, she was allowed to play with her dolls and her beloved King Charles Spaniel dog, named Dash. As she grew older, she loved to paint and draw. She also wrote down her ideas and thoughts in a diary.

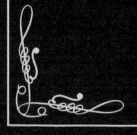

SIR JOHN CONROY

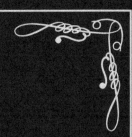

er mother and Sir John Conroy, the comptroller, took her on trips throughout the land. Victoria was about eleven years of age at the time and didn't enjoy these trips. She didn't want to go and couldn't wait to return home. When she was around thirteen, she was told that she might one day be Queen and she remarked that she thought she would make a good one.

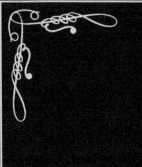

When she was seventeen years of age, her uncle Leopold, who was her mother's brother, brought his nephew Prince Albert to meet Victoria. At the same time, King William brought her a marriage offer from a prince of the Netherlands named Prince Alexander.

QUEEN VICTORIA

PRINCE ALBERT

From the moment she met Albert, who was her cousin, she was fascinated by him.

QUEEN VICTORIA
AND PRINCE ALBERT
AT THE BALL

She wasn't ready to get married yet so they began to share a warm friendship that increased over time.

# QUEEN VICTORIA'S REIGN

After Victoria's uncle, King William IV, passed away, she became the heir to the English throne. She was renamed as Queen Victoria and began ruling in 1837 at the age of eighteen.

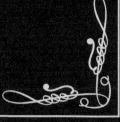

VICTORIA AT HER CORONATION

The formal ceremony of her coronation took place on the 28th of June in 1838 and she was the first Queen to live in Buckingham Palace. She was really too young to make decisions that had world

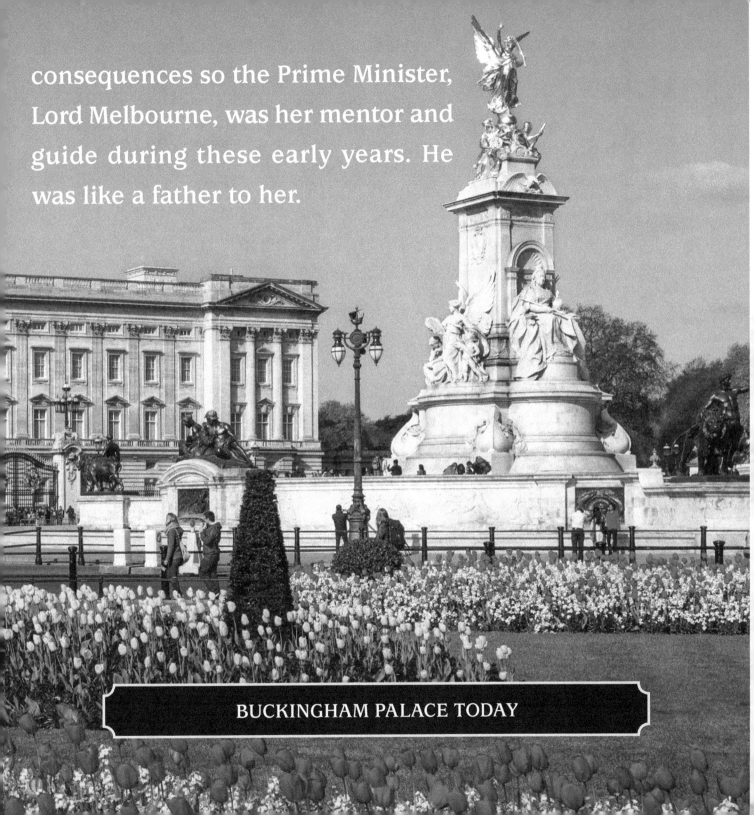

consequences so the Prime Minister, Lord Melbourne, was her mentor and guide during these early years. He was like a father to her.

BUCKINGHAM PALACE TODAY

At the beginning, Victoria was popular among the English citizens, but then she made some critical remarks that involved Lady Flora, one of the ladies-in-waiting at her mother's court. She also made comments about Sir John Conroy. These remarks caused her to be unpopular with her subjects. The bad press led Lord Melbourne to resign his position as Prime Minister, but eventually he was reinstated.

QUEEN VICTORIA, 1837

QUEEN VICTORIA AND PRINCE ALBERT'S WEDDING

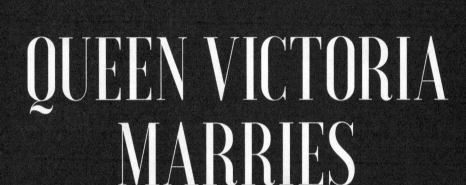

# QUEEN VICTORIA MARRIES

When Albert came back to England in October of 1839, Victoria proposed to him. As Queen, she had to be the one to propose. The two got engaged and then were married on the 10th of February in 1840 at St. James's Palace located in London.

Throughout their lifetimes, Victoria and Albert had nine children together, although she was quoted as saying that she hated being pregnant and wasn't truly fond of children either!

Once the Queen married Albert, Lord Melbourne no longer helped her with decisions. Her husband took that role instead and was forever there at her side as her support. He helped and guided her with all the problems she faced, both political and personal.

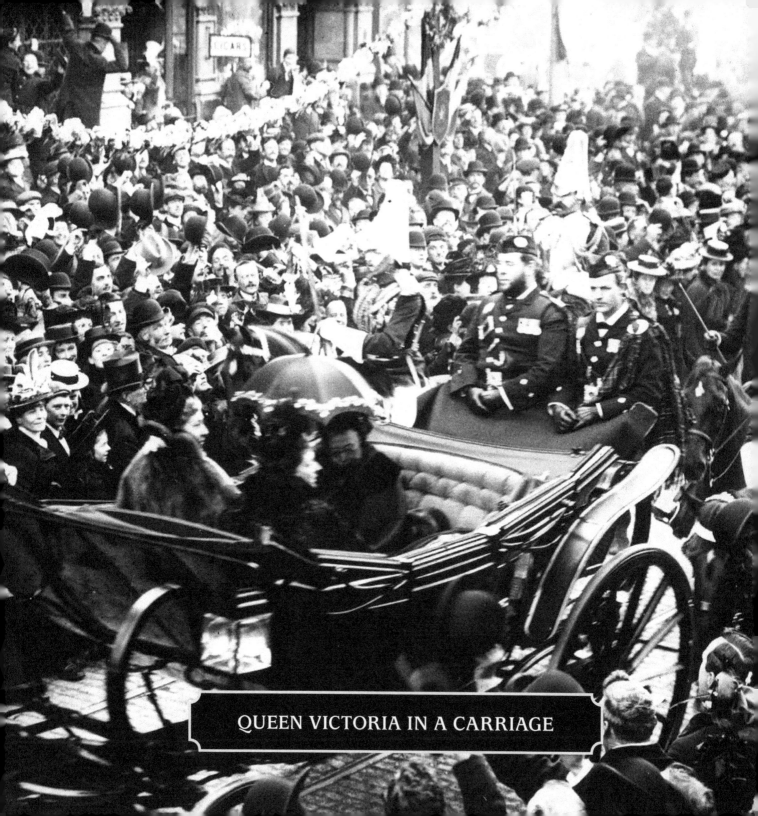

QUEEN VICTORIA IN A CARRIAGE

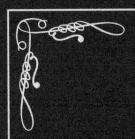

It was a very demanding role being Queen and no matter what decisions she made some segment of the population wasn't happy with the results. During her reign, there were five different attempts to assassinate her and these all occurred when she was traveling in her carriage.

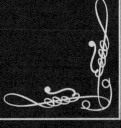

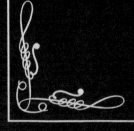
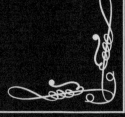

In 1845, the Great Famine happened in Ireland. The Irish farmers depended on potato crops and when the crops were infected with a fungus there was nothing to eat. Sir Robert Peel, who was Prime Minister at the time, sent food to Ireland, but it was not enough. Millions of people passed away or left the country to seek their fortunes elsewhere. Queen Victoria was dubbed the "Famine Queen" during this time. Eventually, Peel resigned and Lord John Russell took his place.

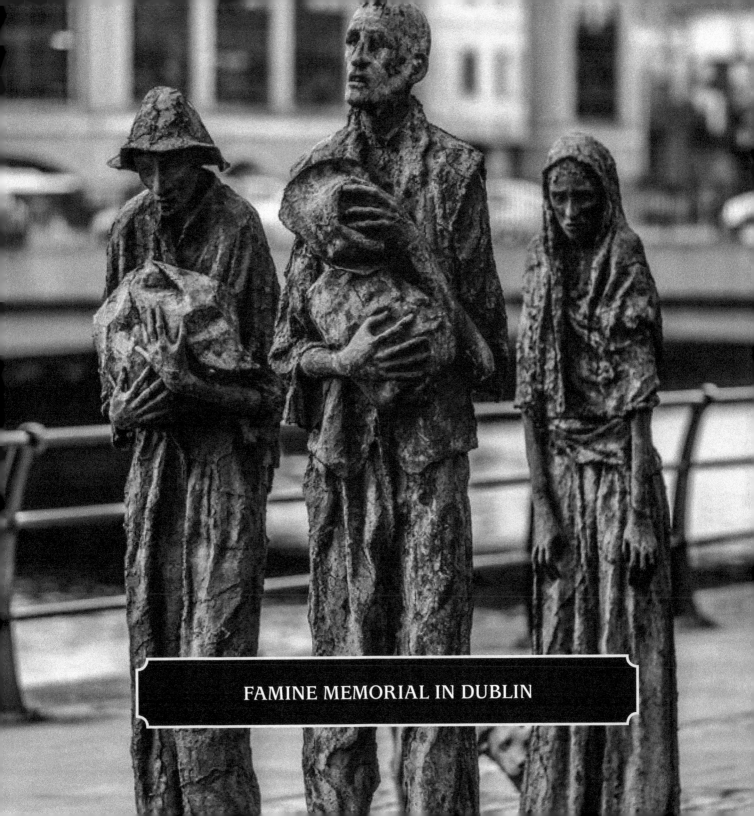

FAMINE MEMORIAL IN DUBLIN

QUEEN VICTORIA VISITING IRELAND

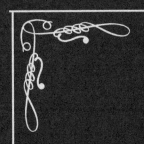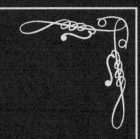

During her reign, Victoria tried to bridge the tense relationship that England had with France. The countries had been at war with each other over many centuries. She arranged for the royal families of Britain and the House of Orleans in France to visit each other. In 1849, she also visited Ireland.

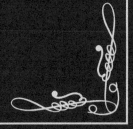

uring Victoria's rule, Britain had an extended period of peace and wealth. It was also a time when there were great strides in industry and transportation. In 1851, Prince Albert, Victoria's husband, worked with Henry

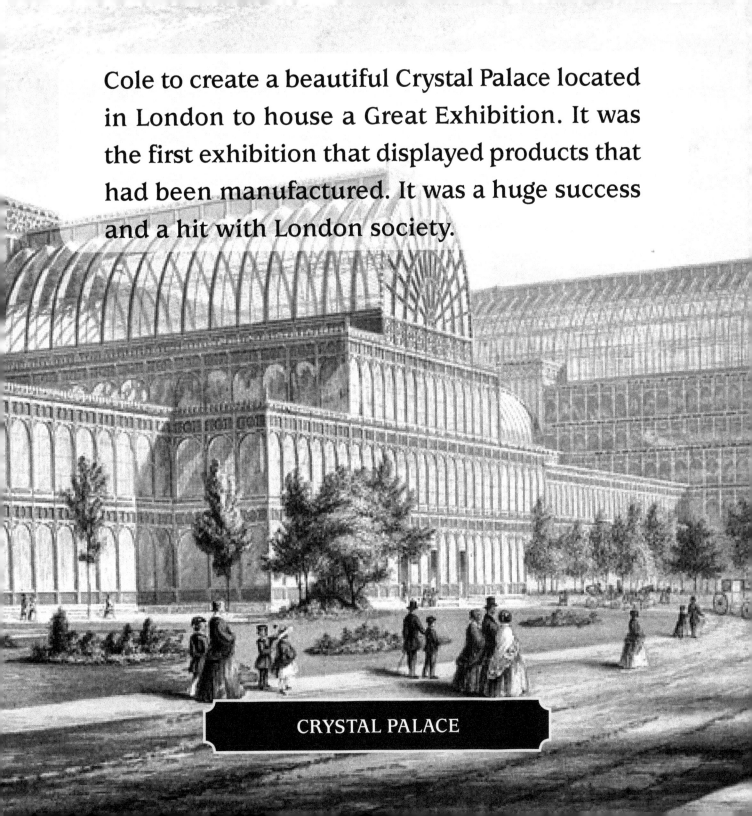

Cole to create a beautiful Crystal Palace located in London to house a Great Exhibition. It was the first exhibition that displayed products that had been manufactured. It was a huge success and a hit with London society.

CRYSTAL PALACE

LORD PALMERSTON

# DIFFERENT PRIME MINISTERS

During Victoria's reign, she had many different Prime Ministers. Unfortunately, the Queen did not get along as well with Lord John Russell as she had with Lord Melbourne and Sir. Robert Peel. As a result, Russell was replaced in 1852. Lord Derby took his place, but by early 1855, Derby was out and Lord Aberdeen was in. Aberdeen didn't keep his power for long. Lord Palmerston was the next Prime Minister.

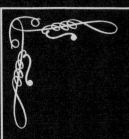
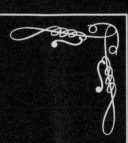

During this time period, Napoleon III, also known as Napoleon Bonaparte, had become close allies with Britain and visited in 1855. When there was an assassination attempt on Napoleon, the friendship that had been established between France and England began to weaken. To strengthen it again, Queen Victoria placed Lord Derby back into his former position at Prime Minister, but it did not last for long. Lord Palmerston was placed in the position again.

NAPOLEON BONAPARTE

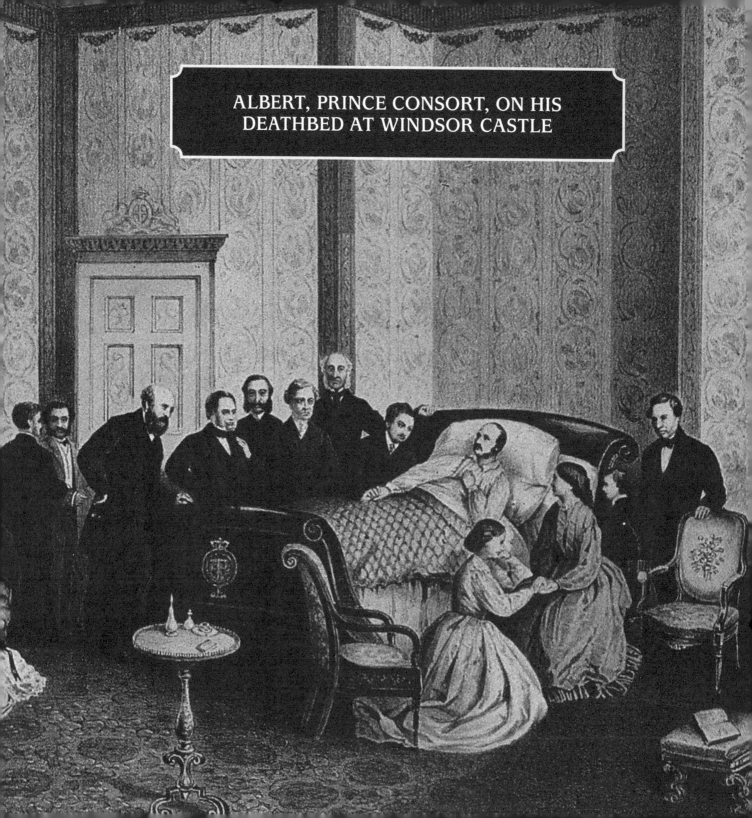

ALBERT, PRINCE CONSORT, ON HIS DEATHBED AT WINDSOR CASTLE

# PRINCE ALBERT'S DEATH

In December of 1861, Prince Albert died from typhoid fever. At that point in time, Queen Victoria and Prince Albert had been married for twenty-one years. She was devastated by his loss and was overcome with grief. She wore black for many years and went into seclusion. She was dubbed the "Widow of Windsor."

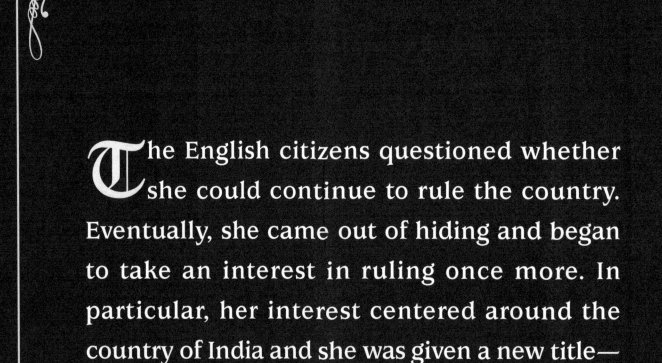

The English citizens questioned whether she could continue to rule the country. Eventually, she came out of hiding and began to take an interest in ruling once more. In particular, her interest centered around the country of India and she was given a new title— Empress of India. Over the years, she became popular with her subjects once more.

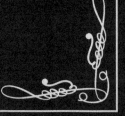

EMPRESS OF INDIA

QUEEN VICTORIA-DIAMOND JUBILEE

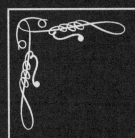

Queen Victoria celebrated her Diamond Jubilee in September of 1896. It was a momentous day in British history since it represented the longest surviving monarchy. There was a long procession to celebrate and an open-air ceremony.

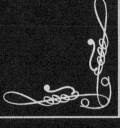

# THE GRANDMOTHER OF EUROPE

Many of Victoria's children married into royalty from other countries so she is often called the "grandmother of Europe." At the time of her death in 1901 at eighty-five years of age, she had over thirty-five great-grandchildren.

QUEEN VICTORIA LYING IN STATE

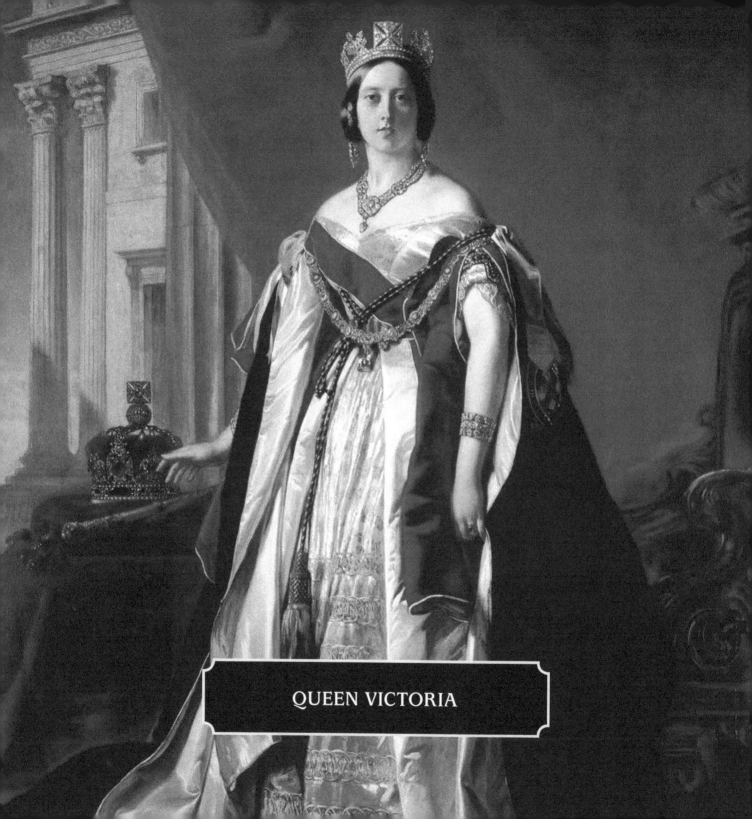

QUEEN VICTORIA

# QUEEN VICTORIA'S REIGN

Queen Victoria became Queen at the age of eighteen and she ruled for 63 years and 7 months, the longest time period of any British monarch to date. Great Britain experienced a great period of expansion and prosperity during her rule.

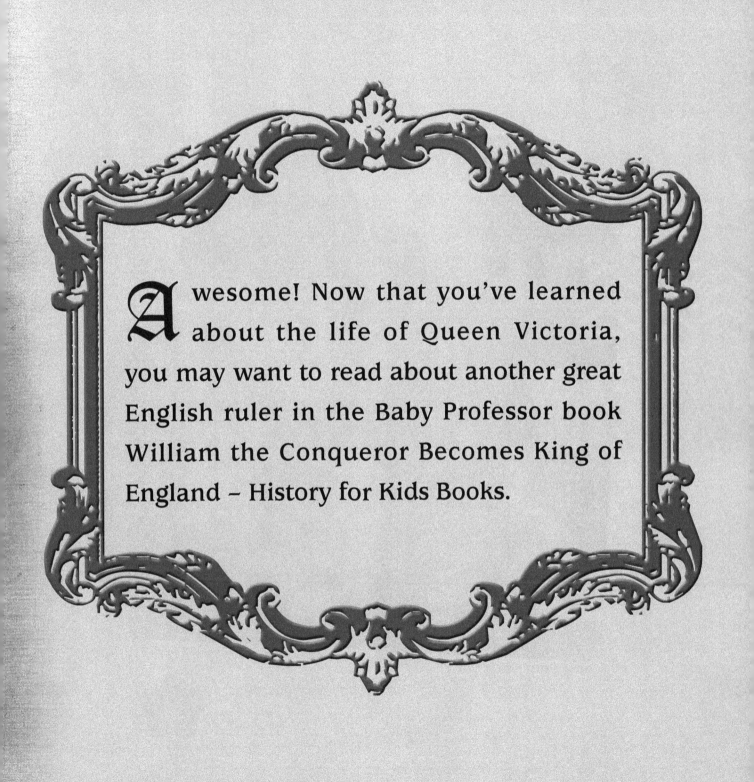

Awesome! Now that you've learned about the life of Queen Victoria, you may want to read about another great English ruler in the Baby Professor book William the Conqueror Becomes King of England – History for Kids Books.

Visit

BABY PROFESSOR
EDUCATION KIDS

# www.BabyProfessorBooks.com

to download Free Baby Professor eBooks
and view our catalog of new and exciting
Children's Books

CPSIA information can be obtained
at www.ICGtesting.com
Printed in the USA
BVHW091551020622
638642BV00004B/458